TOOTING BEC

Best wishes
Janet Smith

CONTENTS

Introduction	3
The Opening Ceremony	6
How the Deal was Done	10
The Royal Connection	14
The Reverend Anderson	15
Early Years	17
The South London Swimming Club	21
The Thirties	26
World War Two and After	30
Modern Times	33
The Future	37

ACKNOWLEDGEMENTS

Many people have helped me in the preparation of this booklet. I should like to thank Anthony Shaw and Meredith Davis at the Local History Library in Battersea for dealing so patiently with my inquiries; the staff at the Greater London Record Office; and at Wandsworth Council. I am also indebted to Shirley Morris, who allowed me to use material from her own records of Tooting, and to Peter Thomas for sharing his research on the Reverend Anderson. My thanks are due to many present and former members of the South London Swimming Club for lending me archive material and talking about their personal experiences of the Lido. I am grateful to Doreen Fitch, Andrew Ingamells, Joan King, Margaret Lipsey and Margy Sullivan for reading the first draft of the manuscript and making some valuable suggestions, many of which appear in the final version. For the use of photographs and other material, I wish to thank: Steve Adkins, George Aldhouse, Jonathan Buckley, Maurice Connor, Ron Elam, Lizzy Hearne, Keith Holdaway, Patrick Loobey, Michael Phillips, Jack Snelling, Egg Sullivan, Yvonne Wood, and Ted Yaxley. I am particularly grateful to Christina Bonnett of Outlines (0171 622 5328) for her cover artwork.

The following organisations have also generously provided photographs.
Greater London Record Office: 4, 6, 7, 8 (Evan Spicer), 12, 27 and 29.
Wandsworth Libraries: 8, 11, 15, 16, and 18.
Imperial War Museum: 30

Designed and typeset by
Hilton Roberts Design: 0171 924 5404

Tooting Bec Lido was first published in Great Britain in 1996 by the South London Swimming Club.

Printed in Great Britain by Battley Brothers Limited, 37 Old Town, Clapham, London SW4 0JN

ISBN 0 9528847 0 4

THE FUTURE – AN UPDATE

In 2006, Tooting Bec Lido celebrated its centenary – a remarkable achievement in an age when lidos have virtually disappeared from the urban landscape.

It is the oldest surviving purpose-built lido in London and is the 3rd oldest in the country. It is also the biggest freshwater lido in Britain.

The South London Swimming Club (SLSC) was formed at Tooting Bec Lido – or Tooting Bathing Lake, as it was originally known – a few weeks after the pool opened in 1906 and it still meets there every Sunday.

In 1996, when this book was published, the SLSC, with the full support of Wandsworth Council, was preparing a bid for Sports Lottery funding.

It became clear, however, that it was unlikely to succeed because of the Fund's reluctance to support open-air pools.

Since then, Wandsworth Council has invested more than £1 million in modernising and repairing the lido.

The most striking change has been the new concrete and glass entrance at the shallow end of the pool, opened in May 2002. Designed by architects W M Martin of London, it was built by Thomas Sinden of Essex.

The original entrance at the south end of the pool still stands.

During the winter of 2006/07, a further refurbishment of the site was carried out by Wandsworth Council. The entire pool tank was relined with blue plastic sheeting, the surrounding paving was renewed and the cubicles were re-roofed and re-painted.

The SLSC works closely with both the Council and D C Leisure, the company now running the lido.

To celebrate the pool's centenary in 2006, the club organised a number of special swimming events and an open-air film festival. In February 2008, it staged the World Cold Water Swimming Championships at the lido, attracting swimmers from around the world.

Janet Smith
February 2008

INTRODUCTION

'We know all the London suburbs, and cannot call to mind any swimming lake like this, 300 feet long, 100 feet wide, and 7 feet deep.' This confident statement appeared in a magazine article on Balham and Tooting in about 1910 - just four years after the Lido had opened. It could still be said today. Tooting Bec Lido remains the largest open-air pool in London and is one of the biggest in Europe.

It was not, however, the first. There were bathing-lakes in many parts of London, including two locally at Clapham and Herne Hill. They were just lakes in parks, but it was partly their popularity that persuaded Wandsworth Borough Council that a swimming-pool should be built on Tooting Common. It was also, at a time of widespread unemployment, a means of providing work for nearly 400 local men.

They and the people of Tooting have one man more than any other to thank for the Lido. He was the Reverend John Hendry Anderson, the rector of St Nicholas Church in Tooting from 1897 to 1913. The Reverend Anderson was a charismatic man with a strong sense of public duty; he was said by one contemporary to be 'a great personality and a whole-hearted champion of the people'. In 1900, he became one of Wandsworth's first councillors, and four years later he was elevated to Mayor. Shortly after his term of office was over, he was elected chairman of the Works Committee of the Central Unemployed Body for London - an early but entirely voluntary Job Centre. There is no doubt that he used his influence with the Central Body to get the Lido built, and there is even a suggestion that it was his idea.

The work began in March 1906 after much wrangling between Wandsworth Borough Council and the London County Council. They finally came to an agreement when the Central Unemployed Body offered to subsidise the project to the tune of £4,000, about half the total cost. At the end of July 1906, the bathing-lake was opened with great fanfare to the public. It was free of charge, but was almost exclusively for the use of men: women were allowed to swim only on Tuesdays.

The hundreds of men and women, who went along to the opening ceremony, knew a very different world to ours. The Liberals were in power, having won a landslide victory in the general election a few months earlier. They had more than twice as many seats as their nearest challengers, the Conservatives. A young

The bathing-lake in Victoria Park, Hackney, 1899

and ambitious Winston Churchill, then a Liberal, was appointed to his first government post as a junior minister for the Colonies. Among the social reforms introduced by the Liberals were old age pensions, though the first payments would not be made until 1909. Also in 1906, the future poet laureate, Sir John Betjeman, was born; the actress, Ellen Terry, was celebrating 50 years on the stage; and the Piccadilly Line on the London Underground was opened. The 'lady with the lamp', Florence Nightingale, was still alive, and the writer, Rudyard Kipling, was about to win the Nobel Prize for Literature. In Rugby Union, England played France for the first time, beating them 35-8 in Paris.

Other important events had not yet happened: the First World War had not broken out; the *Titanic* had not sunk; Louis Bleriot had not flown across the English Channel; the BBC had not broadcast a single programme; and F W Woolworth had yet to open a store. There were fewer than 50,000 cars on the roads (there are now more than 20 million), and what cost an Edwardian 2d would cost us £1.

The history of the Lido is shared by the South London Swimming Club which was formed a few weeks after the bathing-lake opened in 1906. A tradition of early morning swimming whatever the weather soon sprang up and continues today with a small band of swimmers taking to the unheated water every day of the year at around 7.00 am. There is an annual Christmas Day race attracting a mixture of spartan swimmers and baffled onlookers.

The club now runs the Lido on behalf of Wandsworth Council during the winter months - an arrangement that was reached in 1991 to prevent the pool from being closed off-season.

I have been swimming at Tooting Bec Lido for about 5 years and have been a member of the swimming club for two. In that time, I have developed a deep affection for the Lido. I find that swimming in the open-air in such a large pool creates a wonderful feeling of liberation - an experience that is heightened by the simple beauty of the surroundings. Some of my fellow club members have been swimming there for more than 30 years, and a handful for as many as 60.

In writing this booklet, I hope I have captured some of the magic of the Lido and the enthusiasm of its users over 90 years.

THE OPENING CEREMONY

The bathing-lake on Tooting Common was officially opened on the afternoon of July 28th, 1906. It was a Saturday, and evidently hot, for many of the ladies in their long Edwardian dresses shaded themselves from the sun with parasols. The men wore suits and hats, anything from a top-hat to a more casual boater. A band played before and after the speeches, prompting one local paper, the *South Western Star*, to describe the ceremony as 'pretentious'.

The crowd that gathered at the pool-side included dignitaries from the London County Council (LCC) and Wandsworth Borough Council, as well as a large number of local residents. In a photograph of the occasion, one man, who has apparently just walked in, can be seen with his hand over his mouth. Perhaps he was

The opening ceremony with the leading dignitaries on the middle diving board. From L: the Reverend J H Anderson; Alexander Glegg, Mayor of Wandsworth; Stuart Sankey, Chairman LCC Parks and Open Spaces Committee; Evan Spicer, LCC Chairman. July 28th, 1906.

astounded, as many people still are today, by that first sight of the 100 x 33 yard pool.

The borough council had organised and partly funded the scheme on the understanding that the county council would bear the cost of maintaining the bathing-lake once it was finished. The LCC estimated an outlay of about £200 a year; in comparison, the Central Unemployed Body spent £4,200, and Wandsworth Council £3,400 on building the pool.

The Mayor of Wandsworth, Alexander Glegg, formally handed over the bathing-lake to the chairman of the LCC, Evan Spicer. It had been designed by the borough surveyor, H J Marten, and Mr Glegg described it as 'one of the finest of the kind in the whole of London'. He hoped it would be 'a means of affording pleasure, stimulating health and warding off disease'. This last wish would soon be a matter of dispute: within days, there were complaints about rats on the seats; people spitting in the water; and the 'dirty condition of some of the bathers', many of whom walked barefoot across the Common to reach the pool.

With councillors from the LCC present, the Mayor could not resist reminding them of their early reluctance to provide a bathing-lake at all. 'Wandsworth Borough Council

From left to right:

Evan Spicer, Chairman of the London County Council, 1906-07.

Alexander Glegg, Mayor of Wandsworth, 1905-06.

The Reverend John Hendry Anderson, Mayor of Wandsworth, 1904-05. He did more than anyone to ensure that Tooting Bec Lido was built.

went three times to the County Council,' he said, 'in the fashion of an empty-handed lover wooing a coy maiden, and three times their advances were rejected.'

The breakthrough came, Mr Glegg acknowledged, 'largely as a result of the influence and tact of Alderman Anderson', the Wandsworth borough councillor and rector of Tooting who, through his work for the Central Unemployed Body, had been able to provide a workforce.

After the LCC chairman, Mr Spicer, had thanked everyone, it was the turn of the monocled Reverend Anderson. He was a Scot who had come to Tooting nine years earlier, but he was not a newcomer to the parish. His father, the Reverend William Anderson, had left Scotland to become the Presbyterian minister in Tooting, so the young John had spent part of his childhood in what was then a Surrey village. In 1897, he had swapped his living at Foulsham, in Norfolk, with the rector of St Nicholas Church in order to return home.

Standing with the rest of the official party on one of the diving-boards, the Reverend Anderson, who was a noted public speaker, said he was glad that so many were present 'to see what the labours of the unemployed can do.' Yet it was 'very sad to see 391 men who've been employed on that work going back into a labour market that is unable to reabsorb them, with no prospect but to wait until next winter's relief lists are opened.' Even doing that did not guarantee them work: in 1905/06, 31,534 men had registered with their local Distress Committees in London; only 6,392, or one in 5, had found employment.

The Reverend Anderson ended by saying he hoped that the bathing-lake would be 'a benefit to the public for a long time to come.' He can hardly have imagined that ninety years on, local people from Tooting, as well as from many other parts of south London and beyond, would still be swimming in his open-air pool and delighting in it.

After all the speeches, it was finally time for a swim. The man accorded the honour of taking the first official dive into the new lake was the attendant, Alfred French. He was soon followed by hundreds of small boys who, according to the *Wandsworth Borough News,* 'heedless of the presence of members of the fair sex, unblushingly undressed and were sampling the quality of the water long before the 'big guns' had departed.'

For the county councillors, the afternoon was over, but not for the borough councillors. They immediately made their way down to Tooting Broadway for another ceremony, to inaugurate the building of the public baths, which would house slipper baths and showers. They were to be built on the site of the Old Vestry Hall where Homestyle and J. J. Moon's pub now stand. The foundation stone was laid by the Reverend Anderson, and a time capsule was buried on the site.

There had been hopes that an indoor swimming-pool would be built (Tooting was 'crying out for four walls and a tank to swim in', wrote a local journalist). But Tooting would have to wait another 70 years for that.

Bathing Pond
Tooting Bec
Common
Streatham

alfred French
bath attendant
diving after
the Pond was
declared open

28 July 06

The attendant, Alfred French, takes the first official dive into the new lake at about 2.00pm on July 28th, 1906. A year later, he won a Royal Humane Society award for saving two men from drowning.

9

HOW THE DEAL WAS DONE

The Reverend Anderson's key role in securing the outdoor pool for Tooting was acknowledged at the first full council meeting after the opening ceremony. His fellow councillors unanimously passed a resolution thanking him for 'his exertions, both in his capacity as a Member of the Council and as Chairman of the Works Committee of the Central Unemployed Body for London in carrying through the scheme for the provision of the bathing-lake on Tooting Common'. It would, they believed, be of 'great benefit to the inhabitants of the Borough'.

According to one account, the project had been the Reverend Anderson's idea. In an article written many years later, a former editor of the *Tooting & Balham Gazette*, George Hurley, recounted how a procession of unemployed men set off from Church Lane to call in at the Rectory and plead for the Reverend's help. Such a demonstration would not have been an unfamiliar sight to the people of Tooting in the early part of the century. With increasing industrialisation and a rapidly rising population, more and more people were out of work, and there was no welfare state to help them.

Mr Hurley gives no date for the demonstration, but this is his account of what happened:

'The unemployed procession stopped outside the Rectory in Rectory Lane, accompanied by a large crowd, while the Rector saw the leaders. Rumour had it that something stronger than tea was served in the Rectory study during the conference. The result was that the Reverend J H Anderson persuaded the LCC to construct the open-air swimming baths on Tooting Bec Common with local unemployed labour, and the Wandsworth Council also embarked on local unemployment schemes.'

It may have been the Reverend Anderson's idea, but he was not the one to initiate the project. That was done, at an official level at least, by another Wandsworth councillor, John Busfield, on January 6th, 1904. At a council meeting on that day, he put forward a motion calling for the LCC 'to provide an open-air swimming bath on Tooting Common'. The proposal was enthusiastically adopted by the full council.

The LCC was much less enthusiastic. A month later, the Parks and Open Spaces Committee wrote to the borough council to give a distinctly cold response. The councillors had carefully considered the proposal, they said, but found themselves 'unable to do anything in the matter'.

Wandsworth Council was undeterred and unanimously decided to draw up a 'memorial' or petition which was presented to the LCC towards the end of March 1904.

In it, the borough council argued that it was responsible for a large population of more than 250,000 people but had no open-air swimming-bath to offer them, and none was within easy reach. The great success of other lakes, such as those at Brockwell Park and Clapham Common, showed that one on Tooting Common would also be highly appreciated. The need, it went on, had been greatly increased by the LCC's scheme for a housing estate at Totterdown, 'bringing into the borough a large population for whom no baths are provided in their own

Nearly 400 unemployed men were paid 7d an hour to build the lake. Spring 1906.

Spades and wheelbarrows were the main tools used in the construction of Southwark Park boating lake in 1908.

was being considered by the LCC as a means of providing work for the unemployed. Given the Reverend's active role in helping the unemployed, it is impossible not to detect his hand steering events here. The fact that he knew about the discussions before the rest of the council also suggests that he was a party to them. And if the scheme for a bathing-lake had been his own idea, he would have been especially keen to see it realised.

Despite its earlier claim that it had spent enough on bathing facilities, Wandsworth Council now offered to contribute up to £2,000 towards the cost of the lake. It reckoned this would be about a third of the total cost, and clearly hoped that the rest would come from the Central Unemployed Fund and the LCC.

The new situation was set out in two letters to the county council, but to no avail. The LCC said it was not its policy 'to be associated with any expenditure in connection with the provision of work for the unemployed'. For some reason, the decision was not imparted to Wandsworth for another three months when it was told that the LCC was 'not at present prepared to take action' on a bathing-lake.

homes'. Even if you were unable to swim, you could at least have a free bath.

Wandsworth also pointed out that it had spent £40,000 on indoor swimming and bathing facilities in the borough, implying that it was now up to the county council to do its bit. But the LCC baulked at the potential cost, and agreed only to reconsider the matter the following year.

Wandsworth Council was unwilling to wait. In January 1905, the Reverend Anderson (who was by now Mayor of Wandsworth) announced that the councillors' request for an open-air bath

Perhaps the words 'not at present' gave Wandsworth a glimmer of hope. At any rate, it did not give up its campaign, though the next line of attack came not from the borough council itself, but from the Central Unemployed Body for London (CUBL).

In early January 1906, the CUBL (where the Reverend Anderson was newly installed as chairman of the Works Committee) wrote directly to the LCC offering its help in providing a bathing-lake on Tooting Common. The proposal was again dismissed out of hand, but just two weeks later the Parks and Open Spaces Committee changed its mind.

By then, it had received further letters from both Wandsworth Borough Council and the CUBL, and there was probably much else going on behind the scenes. The terms of any deal had now significantly altered. The LCC was no longer being asked to contribute to the cost of building the lake. If it would allow a site to be used on Tooting Common and would agree to maintain the lake, the borough council and 'other sources' (ie the CUBL) would meet the cost of construction.

After more than 2 years of negotiations, the LCC's Parks and Open Spaces Committee agreed to recommend to the full council that Tooting should have its open-air swimming-pool. Wandsworth had suggested a lake of 20,000 square feet, but the LCC stipulated that the pool should not be not less than 30,000 square feet, and that was written into the agreement. Another condition was that a mound, planted with shrubs, should be built around the lake 'in such way that it will not detract from the natural beauty of the Common'. All work would be inspected by the LCC.

There remained the question of whether the county council had the legal authority to allow the borough council to build on the Common. The LCC's solicitor could see no objection, and the formal agreement permitting work to start was signed by council officials on Tuesday, March 13th, 1906. The ceremony was witnessed by Alexander Glegg, Mayor of Wandsworth; Stuart Sankey, Chairman of the LCC's Parks and Open Spaces Committee; and, of course, the Reverend Anderson, on behalf of the Central Unemployed Body.

The CUBL began assigning work to local men on its register. They were to be paid at the rate of 7d (about 3p) an hour for a 43-hour week, giving them a weekly pay packet of 25 shillings (£1.25). Even in 1906, this was precious little, though the CUBL's normal rate of pay for manual labour - in line with that of the LCC - was just 6d an hour. The extra penny was paid because excavating and concreting a lake (and the work appears to have been entirely manual) was recognised as harder than 'levelling and turfing'.

Initially, 145 men were taken on, but by the end of July nearly 400 men had helped to create the bathing-lake. The experience did not appeal to all of them. More than 70 gave up the job shortly after starting. Some were not fit enough for the work, but one man claimed that he was 'nervous of water'. The first task, of clearing the site, began on Monday, March 19th, 1906.

THE ROYAL CONNECTION

Princess Alexandra of Denmark married the Prince of Wales (later King Edward VII) in 1863 when she was only 19. Her beauty and grace were said to have captivated the heart of the nation. Portrait by Sir Luke Fildes, 1883.

Why did the LCC suddenly abandon its opposition to the bathing-lake? The answer may lie in the account-books of the Central Unemployed Body.

The organisation, which was run by volunteers to help the unemployed in London, was funded from two sources: the rates and voluntary contributions.

Between November 1905 and the end of March 1906, the income from a levy on rates amounted to just over £1,500. Donations from the public, on the other hand, totalled more than £47,000. The bulk of this - over £45,000 - came from the Queen's Unemployed Fund.

The Fund had been set up by the government in late 1905 in an attempt to tackle the growing problem of unemployment. It was headed by Queen Alexandra, the popular consort of Edward VII, who was concerned at the desperate plight of the thousands of people out of work. In November, she had made an appeal to the public for money, and in little over a month, £125,000 had been raised. A large share of this found its way to the Central Unemployed Body: by July 1906 it had received nearly £64,000.

So during the winter and spring of 1905/06, the CUBL had a huge amount of money at its disposal. As chairman of the Works Committee, the Reverend Anderson must have known this, and must also have realised that such manna from heaven was unlikely to fall again. He surely used this knowledge to persuade the hesitant county councillors that here was a chance not to be missed. The LCC could, in effect, have a bathing-lake on the cheap, but only if it acted quickly.

THE REVEREND ANDERSON

Once work on the bathing-lake had started, the CUBL kept a close eye on its progress. The organisation was run by high-minded and well-intentioned men, but their reports appear rather patronising. The unemployed were described as 'a mixed lot', who were 'unable to do a fair day's work owing to weakness, and time has to be given them to pull themselves together'. Nonetheless, they were deemed on the whole to be 'favourable representatives of the class to which they belong'. Working on Tooting bathing-lake appears to have been beneficial. The CUBL approvingly reported that the men 'improved in physique, capacity and zeal'.

The energetic Reverend Anderson himself made a point of visiting the site on Tooting Common. It was on Friday, May 4th, 1906, at about the half-way stage in the building work. His assessment was almost gleeful: he told fellow-members of the CUBL a few days later that he was 'specially pleased with the splendid work' that was being done there.

The Reverend Anderson's reputation as a champion of the poor had been assured in 1902 when he intervened in a council debate to oppose a ban on beer at Coronation Dinners in honour of Edward VII. The new king had offered £30,000 to

The Reverend John Hendry Anderson. Rector of Tooting, 1897-1913. This photograph was published shortly after his death on November 11th 1913 and was available from a local photographer for 2d.

pay for a formal meal for 500,000 of his 'poorer subjects' in London. He also suggested that two cups of ale (about three-quarters of a pint) should be served to allow the guests to drink the king's health, if they wished. The arrangements for the dinner - to be held on Saturday, July 5th - were left in the hands of the mayors of each borough. In Wandsworth, a Coronation Celebration Committee was set up (yes, the Reverend Anderson was on it), and a King's Dinner Sub-Committee.

The Coronation Dinner at Tooting Graveney School, July 5th, 1902. The Coronation itself was postponed because Edward VII was ill, but the celebrations in Wandsworth went ahead as planned.

The former agreed that beer should be served, but the latter voted overwhelmingly against it.

At a heated debate to settle the issue, the Reverend Anderson was one of several councillors to speak in favour of providing beer. He said he had come to the meeting to 'raise his voice for liberty and against tyranny'. He might be a clergyman, but he would 'rather see Wandsworth free than Wandsworth sober'. He revealed that earlier in the day he had ordered three-quarters of a pint of Bass's ale. 'I drank the beverage,' he said, 'indeed, I did not leave a drop in the glass. And I must confess that as I walked down Pall Mall afterwards, I formed a very high opinion of Bass's ale.' He could see no reason why the poor should not be allowed to celebrate with a glass of beer, and he won the day.

The Reverend's work for the Central Unemployed Body, which met twice a month, and for Wandsworth Council, where at one stage he sat on three committees, inevitably kept him away from his parish for much of the time. As an outspoken man with a high public profile he attracted many critics. They felt he was more interested in municipal matters than his clerical duties, but the Reverend Anderson was unconcerned. 'They expect', he said, 'that I ought to go about with a basin of pea-soup in one hand and a Bible in the other; but that is not my idea of benefiting my fellow man.'

In early 1913, he suffered the devastating blow of the loss of his seventeen-year old only daughter, Elspeth. At about the same time, he badly injured himself in a fall down a flight of cellar steps. The Reverend Anderson never recovered and died on November 11th, 1913. More than five thousand people are reported to have been at his funeral at St Nicholas Church. Among the many floral tributes on his grave was one which bore the message: 'In sincere condolence, from the Balham road-sweepers, who have lost a good and true friend.'

EARLY YEARS

The new bathing-lake was instantly popular. The hundreds of small boys who were 'disporting themselves in the water to their hearts' content' in the first half-hour that the pool was open were the first of thousands, if not millions, of swimmers to do so. Official attendance figures recorded over a 12-week period in the summer of 1908 show that more than 112,000 swims were taken - about 1,500 a day. Even during the hot summer of 1995, just over half that number was recorded: 65,917.

Not everyone was enchanted, though, and there were soon complaints about the personal hygiene of some of the bathers. Just three days after the pool had opened, a Mr Davis from Streatham wrote to the borough council: 'I and several friends who are ratepayers would be glad to avail ourselves of a swim in this splendid bath, but not after the greater majority of such as those I saw there yesterday.' Another local resident said he was 'unable to enjoy a bathe in company with boys and men who are filthy both in clothes and person.' Yet another complained that the bathing-lake was being 'stormed by the riff-raff from slum-land'.

Other users were appalled at the amount of spitting. 'It should be absolutely prohibited in the water', one man told the county council, 'but it [spit] is found floating on the water, and over the whole of the cement surrounding the bath.' The other main cause for complaint was rats. One bather described his disgust when he picked up his wet costume and 'found that it was covered with vermin.' Another man also complained about the rats, saying that one of his friends, a chemist, 'considers the existing state of things too filthy to avail himself of the bath.'

The lake was a simple structure with none of the additional facilities that are so much a part of the Lido today. There was no cafe, no fountain, and there were no brightly coloured cubicle doors. In fact, there were no cubicles. Instead, there was just a primitive shelter with a corrugated iron roof down one side of the pool, the eastern side, next to the railway line. Within two years, the county council realised that it was 'quite inadequate for the accommodation of the enormous number of bathers in the lake'. In the summer of 1908, a second shelter - also without doors - was erected along the opposite side of the pool.

It did not matter that there was no privacy for changing because mixed bathing was not allowed. The lake was largely for the use of men and boys, who were able to swim every day of the week from 6.00 am

At first the bathing-lake had open changing accommodation and a boat for rescues. 1906/7.

The diving-boards with attendant, Alfred French, 2nd on right, c.1912. The boards were dismantled in the 1970s for safety reasons.

onwards. Women and girls, on the other hand, were restricted to Tuesdays after 8.30 am. The pool was closed each day between 11.00 am and 2.00 pm, and on Sundays swimming finished at 9.00 am. Soon, an hour was set aside in the middle of the day for swimming-lessons for schoolchildren.

It was clearly a raw deal for women but pre-First World War life was far from equal. The suffragette movement was becoming increasingly militant, but all women over the age of 21 would not get the vote until 1928. Of the 112,000 swims recorded in the summer of 1908, 105,000 were taken by men and just 3,000 by women. This glaring imbalance was largely because the pool was available to women on only 15 days in the 3 months in question, compared with 87 days for the men. (The remaining 4,000 swims are accounted for by children, with the boys taking three times as many as the girls.) In 1907, 54 local women signed a petition asking the LCC to allow them to use the pool on 3 afternoons a week, but their plea was ignored.

There were two features at the bathing-lake that no longer exist. In front of the attendant's office, there was an imposing 3-tier set of diving boards which had provided a ready-made podium for the opening ceremony. The boards lasted many years, finally being dismantled in the Seventies when it was thought unwise to allow people to dive into just 7 feet of water.

Another special feature was a rowing-boat. It was generally moored at the deep end and was intended to make it easier to rescue swimmers in difficulties in the middle of the pool. The original boat had been borrowed from another park, but in October 1906 a Mr Winter provided Tooting bathing-lake with one of its own for £18 5s (£18.25).

The water itself was soon causing alarm. As early as 1907, there were complaints that the bottom of the pool was covered in mud and slime. The LCC had only itself to blame. When the lake was under construction, it had ignored a suggestion that a pair of Bell's Filters should be installed at a cost of around £600. Now the council decided that the pool would have to be emptied and cleaned each year. This was done for the first time in March 1908, at a cost of £25. When the same procedure was carried out in May 1996, the cost was nearly £2,500.

An annual spring clean was not, of course, enough. A man who swam at the pool during the First World War, 85 year old Maurice Connor, recalls that the water used to be black. 'You couldn't see the bottom of the pool', he says, 'not even in the shallow end.' And Hazel Green, who was taken as a child to the Lido in the late Twenties, remembers that it was impossible to stand up in the water, 'you just slithered on the bottom.'

Dirty water was not peculiar to Tooting Bec. In 1928, at Southwark Park bathing-lake an 8 year old girl drowned but, because of the state of the water, nobody noticed her body. It was only found the following day when the police were called in to drag the pool.

Although there was no cafe at the pool-side in Tooting in 1906, there was a refreshment hut outside the perimeter fence, near the entrance. At first, it was only a tent, but by the second summer a small wooden building with a pitched roof was built to meet the needs of 'the large number of persons who use the bathing-lake'. The licensee was Albert Ruby, who also ran the refreshment house on Tooting Common and another at Ravenscourt Park. His price-list from Ravenscourt Park survives, and it is fair to assume that he charged much the same at Tooting. The food and seating area were divided into first and second-class:

	1st	2nd
Tea, coffee, cocoa	2d	1d
Chocolate	3d	-
Cake	2d	1d
Fancy pastries	2d	-
Cold meat or ham	6d	-
Boiled egg	2d	-
Mineral water	2d	1d
Cigarettes (10)	3d	3d

The first chapter in the Lido's life came to an end with the outbreak of the First World War in 1914. The pool stayed open throughout the War, but since it was very much a male preserve, it must have been uncannily quiet.

Albert Ruby's refreshment house on Tooting Common, c.1907.

THE SOUTH LONDON SWIMMING CLUB

The South London Swimming Club, like the swimming-pool, came into being in the summer of 1906. A group of swimmers who met at the bathing-lake decided to band together to organise races and give lessons. The club's formal objectives were 'to provide tuition in swimming and diving, to promote classes for teaching life-saving and to encourage healthy exercise and social intercourse'. There were about 20 members - now there are more than 500. Two years later, the LCC agreed that the club could use the bathing-lake, or the Bec, as it came to be known, as its headquarters. It still is today.

To begin with, it was an all-male club. Women were not allowed to join until 1931. They were always made welcome at social events, especially if they were willing to do the catering, but club membership was another matter. The issue of their status had been discussed at the annual general meeting in 1930, but the men had voted decisively against admitting them. One argument was that mixed bathing was still not allowed at the pool, so there was no point in having women members. Another, put forward by a senior club member, was that the ladies 'did everything for love of the club, they would do it willingly whether they had a label tied round their necks or not.' A year later,

when mixed bathing was introduced at the pool, the decision was reversed, and 62 women (dubbed the 'Bec Mermaids' in the local press) immediately joined the club. Now, there are just over 200 women members, and 300 men.

The club laid great emphasis on life-saving, so it is hardly surprising that it should have taken such pride in its captain, William Laws, when in 1930 he won a Royal Humane Society award for saving a woman from drowning. The incident had happened in the summer at Sonning-on-Thames. Mr Laws managed to rescue the woman, who had suffered a heart attack and was clinging on to another swimmer, putting them both in danger. When he received his award from the Mayor of Wandsworth, the modest Mr Laws, who was captain of the SLSC for 22 years, talked not about himself or his heroic deed but about the club: 'We do not go in to win prizes or produce fast swimmers ... What we do is to teach swimmers to swim well, and then when they can, we try to induce them to take a course of life-saving instruction...'

The club's commitment to teaching has always been strong. It became apparent that an unheated outdoor pool was not an ideal venue and, at different times, the

Rose Merritt ignores snow and ice to take a dip. Early 1970s.

Christmas Day race, 1921.

indoor pools at Streatham, Norbury and
Balham have been used instead.
Nowadays, the SLSC holds its weekly
classes at Clapham Manor Baths, where
the club President, Bob Pattison, and a
team of instructors put children and adults
through their paces. Life-saving classes are
also given at a local school .

From the outset, the club has held regular
races and competitions at the Bec. In the
late Twenties, one club member provided
what seemed like an unlimited supply of
silver spoons, and these were offered as
prizes in fortnightly competitions. The
races were generally held on Wednesdays

at 7.15 or 7.30 am before the competitors
went to work. Occasionally, there were so
many participants that heats had to be
organised with a final on the Saturday
morning.

The silver spoons have long since run out
but a weekly race is still held on Sunday
mornings at the Lido. The prize is often a
silver cup or salver, many of them donated
by past club members, which the winner
holds for a year. The races, over different
distances according to the time of year and
the temperature of the water, are
handicapped to ensure a fair share of the
spoils.

The races continue throughout the winter months, and there has never been a shortage of swimmers willing to break the ice. At a club dinner in January 1932, the heroic captain, Mr Laws, drank a toast to 'all those who went swimming last Wednesday morning when their towels froze'. About 20 members rose to their feet to respond.

The Christmas Day race is a tradition that is as old as the club. It is an event for the hardy - or some would say, the foolhardy. It is also an entertaining sight for the spectators, many of them wrapped up in thick winter coats while the swimmers dive into the icy water in skimpy costumes. The Burton Cup, awarded to the winner of the men's race (two widths), is one of the club's most coveted trophies. In 1931, it was won by a young and athletic Douglas Mann. 'The colder the water, the better he likes it', commented the report in the *Balham and Tooting News & Mercury*. Mr Mann was to remain a club member for 65 years; by the time of his death in late 1995 at the age of 84, he was the longest-serving member on record.

The ladies' Christmas Day race is over the shorter distance of one width. It was won in 1995 by Yvonne Wood who, at the age

Bottom left, Derrick Berry is presented with the Burton Cup after winning the Christmas Day race, 1948. Nearly fifty years later, his sister, Yvonne Wood (below), wins the cup for the ladies' Christmas Day race, 1995.

had a reputation for strictness which is reflected in the minutes of a 1958 club meeting:

> 'Mr Willis reported on progress which he did not consider satisfactory. He thought that some of the more irresponsible members, by their rowdiness, were impeding those with a genuine desire to improve their swimming...'

His son, Jerome Willis, recalls being taken to the Lido as a boy in the Thirties, and 60 years on, he still swims there when he can. *His* daughter, Megan, who first swam at the Lido with her grandfather, is now one of 4 trustees of the club. She is happy to be continuing a family tradition begun 70 years ago: 'The Lido is a community facility that I hugely enjoy', she says, 'and I want to make sure it's there for future generations.'

of 73, completed a notable family hat-trick of Christmas Day victories. Her eldest brother, Derrick Berry, won the Burton Cup twice in the Thirties and Forties and her younger brother, Jack, also went on to win it. Not to be outdone, her husband, Cyril Wood, who has been swimming at the Lido for more than 60 years, has also won it three times.

There is an equally bone-chilling race on New Year's Day. In a handicapped race, men and women compete for the Willis Cup, given to the club in memory of Bob Willis by his widow. He was the first of three generations of his family to join the SLSC, and a fourth is already dipping its toes into the Lido. Mr Willis Senior joined in 1926, and was still a member at the time of his death 50 years later. For many years, he was Chief Swimming Instructor, and

One of the club's longest serving ice-breakers is Bob Fitch, who first swam at Tooting Bec Lido in 1929 when he was a boy. Now in his mid-seventies and recovering from a stroke, he still gets up early, in summer and winter, to start the day with a swim. 'It makes me feel great', he says, 'and the Lido helped me to get over diabetes and a stroke better than the doctors did.'

In the late Twenties, an annual river swim was started. As its name suggests, it originally took place in the Thames. The men raced over a course of one mile, downstream from Walton-on-Thames, and the women over half-a-mile. The race is still held every year, but in the more hygienic waters of the Lido. One tradition that has now lapsed is the annual sea swim which, from the Thirties onwards, took place at resorts such as Brighton, Littlehampton, and Bognor Regis. It was an opportunity for members to pit themselves against each other and the swell of the sea - at Brighton racing between the piers.

Perhaps the most enterprising club members were the South London Four whose reputation for fine swimming and thrilling stunts made them local celebrities in the Thirties. The Four were: William Downing, J. H. Lofthouse, R. E. Lowe and Horace Lock. In 1932 alone, they took part in 50 displays. By the following year, Mr Downing had perfected his Count of Monte Cristo act, which he performed at Streatham Baths. The account in the *Balham & Tooting News & Mercury* is hair-raising:

> 'Handcuffed, with his feet tied, and then placed in a sack, which was tied up at the top and set alight, he dived into the water. There was an anxious moment while he remained submerged, but there were sighs of relief and exclamations of delight and appreciation when he reappeared, minus his handcuffs, bonds and sack, and with a very devilish change of costume.'

The SLSC no longer has a daredevil team performing such stunts, but it has an extraordinary number of long-serving

A sideways look at winter swimmers by amateur cartoonist and SLSC member, Ted Yaxley.

members who have an unswerving devotion to the Lido. Many speak of the sense of well-being engendered by the open space, the blue water, the surrounding trees, and the intense exhilaration of swimming in cold water. Another attraction is the absence of noise that bounces round an indoor pool.

The oldest club member is 93-year old Henry Harvey who, until recently, swam 2 widths every day of the summer. Not far behind is 87-year old Charles Bacon, who joined the SLSC when he retired nearly 20 years ago and now comes regularly to the Lido. 'It's a unique place', he says, offering 'peace and tranquillity away from the hustle and bustle of life.'

THE THIRTIES

If there was one decade in which Tooting Bec Lido flourished more than any other it was the Thirties. It was a golden era for lidos generally. They were a top priority for the LCC which, in 1935, planned to build 9 more in London. The outbreak of war in 1939 interrupted the programme, but by then 4 had already opened: at Victoria Park (May 1936); Brockwell Park (July 1937); Parliament Hill Fields (August 1938) and Charlton (May 1939). Some borough councils provided their own lidos and others were built outside the capital.

People had more leisure time than ever before. For many, it was enforced idleness through unemployment; in the middle of the decade, a sixth of the working population was without a job. For those in work, however, conditions were steadily improving. The average working-week for a manual labourer was down to less than 48 hours, and by the end of the decade 11 million people were allowed one week's annual holiday with pay.

The leisure industry was expanding and more sports facilities were being provided. The authorities also encouraged people to be physically fit - a goal that was much in vogue in Germany and Italy at the same time. In the summer of 1939,

Wandsworth Council organised a Fitness and Health Rally at Wandsworth Stadium. There were demonstrations of boxing, weight-lifting, wrestling, gymnastics and keep fit exercises. The *Wandsworth Borough News* reported that 'men, women and children from all over Wandsworth stood in a blazing sun, perspiring in the cause of physical fitness.' They heard Lord Aberdare, the chairman of the National Fitness Council, say in a morale-boosting speech that 'in work or play, fitness wins.'

During the Thirties, the word 'lido' (from the Italian for 'sea-shore') was increasingly used for outdoor pools. They were places where you could almost imagine you were at the seaside. You could swim, do exercises, play games or just sun-bathe, and most lidos had a cafe so that ice-creams and drinks were also available. Lidos were ideal destinations for a family day-out, especially for those who could not afford to go away on holiday.

There was also a fashion for sun-bathing and being in the open air. It was long before any worries about a hole in the ozone layer and the harmful effects that the sun's rays could have.

Alterations carried out at Tooting Bec in 1931 were substantial. The most

Brockwell Park Lido, 1939.

important was the installation of filtration plant to ensure that the water stayed clean. An aerator, or fountain, was also built at the shallow end of the pool to help pump the water round. These improvements had already been carried out at most of the LCC's outdoor pools; Tooting was the last to be upgraded.

The filtration plant brought with it two other significant changes: mixed bathing and an entry charge. The LCC had decided in 1927 to allow mixed bathing at 2 of its open-air pools, and it proved so popular that the concession was gradually extended, but only to pools that had proper water cleaning equipment. At the same time, the council introduced a charge of 6d (less than 3p) per adult and 3d (just over 1p) per child at mixed bathing times. This was largely to help pay for a female attendant.

Until now, the dressing accommodation had consisted of open shelters on either side of the pool. A canvas curtain was fitted to the front of them for anyone overcome by modesty. With the prospect of mixed bathing, the LCC decided to build more cubicles on both sides and to fit doors to the existing shelters. More cubicles were again added in 1936 when the cafe - such a distinctive feature of lidos of this period - was also built.

To begin with, mixed bathing was allowed only on early closing-days, Sundays and Bank Holidays. It was accompanied by a host of rules and regulations. The men, who preferred to strip off in the open air, now had to change in the cubicles. Those on the railway side of the pool were for men, and the ones opposite for women. There were also rules about clothing. Women were not allowed to wear two-piece swim-suits, though many got round the edict by fastening a piece of string or even a shoe-lace between the two halves and claiming it was one costume.

For the men, who had held sway at the Lido since its opening in 1906, it was a dramatic change. A long-time member of the South London Swimming Club, Charles Roskilly, expressed his frustration in verse:

In days of old, at Tooting Lake, (Deny it, if you
  can),
Away from toil, from care, from home,
A man could be a MAN,
For FREEDOM was the watchword then,
And FREE MEN gathered there,
While hearts were young and hopes were high
In Tooting sun and air.

Alas! One day the LCC,
Those mighty powers that be,
Said 'We'll improve your bath for you
And do the whole thing free.'
They built a big filtration plant,
The sides like glass did shine,
And after many a month, behold!
A super Serpentine!

So now we have our comforts and
The water's always clear,
We've Rules and Regulations, too,
With penalties severe.
Within a nasty wooden hutch
Swimmers remove their clothes.
Without a permit signed and sealed
A man can't blow his nose.

We can't do this; we can't do that,
The LCC say 'No'.
We can't dress here, we can't dress there,
In cages we must go.
The lake was built for honest men,
But we're becoming slaves.
The LCC rules swimmers though
Britannia rules the waves.

Beware the swimmers' awful wrath;
One day we'll sound the call.
With shouts of joy, through streets of blood,
We'll march on County Hall.
We'll tear the place down stone by stone,
We'll throw it in the sea;
We'll burn all regulations, and
Once more we shall be FREE.

Mr Roskilly would have celebrated the demise of the LCC in 1965 when its powers were handed over to the Greater London Council. It was not until 1971, when the GLC delegated some of its powers to the borough councils, that Wandsworth became responsible for the Lido.

These changes in local government have not, however, brought an end to the regulations, and rules on safety are probably stricter than ever before. Diving, for instance, is no longer allowed at the Lido. And as recently as 1993, there was a row when a manager at the pool asked a woman, who was sunbathing topless, to cover up. The council afterwards admitted that it did not have the power to stop topless sunbathing, but said it was not something that it wanted to encourage.

WORLD WAR TWO AND AFTER

Mitcham Road in Tooting was damaged in an air-raid in November 1940.

Throughout the Second World War, Tooting Bec Lido stayed open - as it had done during the First World War - but this time the fighting came much nearer to home.

Anti-aircraft guns and barrage balloons were positioned on Tooting Bec Common, close to the Lido. The site itself (like all the LCC's open-air pools) was earmarked by the government for use as a

first-aid post and was also put at the disposal of the National Fire Service.

The Lido did not suffer a direct hit, even though south-west London came under numerous bombing attacks. In 1940, German warplanes started dropping bombs on Streatham and Tooting; then in 1944, came the V1 flying bombs or 'doodlebugs', and they were followed a year later by V2 rockets. Several bombs fell on Aldrington Road directly opposite the pool, and so many landed in Streatham that it was known for a time as 'doodlebug alley'. Throughout the borough of Wandsworth - which at that time included Clapham and Streatham, but not Battersea - more than 1,000 people were killed and more than 2,000 were seriously injured; widespread damage to property meant that 10,000 people had to be re-housed.

There was some blast damage to the buildings at the Lido and the LCC allocated £1,000 for repairs and refurbishment once the war was over.

The SLSC's Bob Fitch, who had already been going to the Lido for 10 years by the outbreak of war, remembers swimming there with shrapnel falling all around him. Nothing seems to have stopped this quietly determined man from using the pool. Even on his wedding-day in 1943, he made sure that he had a swim at the Lido before going to the church. More than fifty years later, he and his wife, Doreen, are still married and are still active members of the club.

After the war, the SLSC, like many other clubs, went through a lean spell. The country had more pressing priorities than sport and inevitably there were club members who did not return from the war. By the end of 1952, the SLSC was in the red, and there was concern at the shortage of members in the 20-35 age range.

It was at about this time that a new and energetic intake of members arrived on the scene. They included Joe Blanchard, a French diplomat who lived just a few hundred yards from the pool. He claims not to have known of its existence for the first 2 years that he was there. Then, one day in 1955, he spotted 'people walking along with a towel on one shoulder and on the other a swim-suit'. He followed them and discovered the Lido hidden away behind a cluster of trees on Tooting Common. There are still many people living within walking distance of the pool who are surprised to find it for the first time.

Mr Blanchard soon became friends with Doug Smith, whose talents, apart from being an accomplished swimmer, included speaking French. Mr Smith's widow, Renee, says that the two men 'formed an Anglo-French friendship and made plans to make a brighter future for the club and its members'. She adds: 'I would not like to count the many bottles of wine to put this plan into action.' With the help of others, they organised charity galas and outings, took a group of children to Paris to compete against a French club, and encouraged more people to join the SLSC. 'The aim', Mr Blanchard says, was to create 'a friendly club rather than a tip-top swimming club.'

One of his youngest recruits was Bob Pattison, who joined the SLSC in the mid-Fifties when he was 9 years old and who is now the club President. He astonished older hands by swimming through his first winter - a feat recently emulated by his daughter, Louise, who at 12 years old is already a regular winter swimmer.

In the Fifties, a number of new groups, whose primary interest was not in swimming, began to use the Lido and formed the Bec Physical Culture Club. They included weight-lifters, gymnasts and runners. One of the newcomers was George Aldhouse, a meat-cutter at Smithfield Market, who would spend long hours practising acrobatics with a group of friends. He later joined the SLSC and retired as Honorary Handicapper in 1996 after 25 years of keeping order at the weekly Sunday race.

George Aldhouse (in white trunks) and friends practise their balancing act. Early 1950s.

MODERN TIMES

Recent developments at the Lido have been brought about largely by changes in local government. When the pool was handed over to Wandsworth in 1971, the council had a Labour majority. The Recreation Committee immediately embarked on a survey of its newly acquired sites and concluded that many of the amenities were 'in a run-down state and badly in need of improvement'. It recommended that Tooting Bec Lido should have updated pumping equipment, new dressing accommodation and a modernised entrance, at a cost of £800,000 (later pared down to £300,000). Nonetheless, it was a low priority and by the time work should have started, Labour had lost power to the Conservatives.

Under the Tories, the new watchword was 'efficiency'. In 1979, the council set itself a target of achieving savings of £450,000. An outdoor pool that was largely used only in the summer was an obvious target. The council decided to close the Lido in the winter and save itself more than £6,000. It was not alone in seeing lidos as expensive luxuries. Throughout the Eighties and early Nineties, many lidos in London and elsewhere were closed on grounds of cost. Among them was Wandsworth's only other open-air pool, the Big Splash at King George's Park.

Bob Fitch, a regular at the Lido for more than sixty years.

The council's plans for Tooting Bec Lido would initially have hit only the stalwarts of the SLSC but there were fears that once it closed, it would never re-open. The club organised a petition, which was signed by a thousand people, and sought a meeting with the council.

The delegation was led by the veteran club member, Bob Fitch, who made an impassioned plea for the Lido to remain open throughout the year. In his efforts to convince the council that the Lido was a necessity of life for many people, he came close to accusing councillors of conspiracy to murder:

> 'The Bec community will move outside the Borough for their outdoor swim - except the elderly, of course, who will be so shattered one can only ponder on how you will be shortening their lives.'

He also argued that if the Lido were unattended for 9 months of the year, it would be damaged by vandals, and the unbroken ice would crack the concrete pool. The council would end up with an expensive repair bill, making closure a false economy.

The council agreed to think again. It was decided that the Lido would close for only 2 days a week during the winter season, but the concession allowing free early morning swimming would be ended.

The Lido is emptied and cleaned out at a cost of nearly £2,500. May 1996.

Instead, club members would have to buy a £30 annual season ticket which they could use at the Lido or any other swimming-pool in the borough.

Throughout the Eighties, when the Conservatives retained control of Wandsworth, more and more council services were privatised. By the end of the decade, it was the turn of the leisure services. In 1989, an in-house management team, Direct Services Organisation, won the first contract for a 5-year term. After the next round of tendering in 1994, the contract went to Civic Leisure Ltd, this time, for 6 years. At

the Lido, Civic are responsible for the quality of the water and the plant, as well as the day-to-day management of the site during the summer; however, the council retains overall charge of the facility, including maintenance of the buildings and the pool itself.

A more commercial approach to the Lido meant that in 1991 it was again threatened with closure during the winter. As in 1979, the SLSC reacted with alarm fearing a total shut down as the eventual outcome. A 'Save the Lido' committee was formed, and a delegation of 4 club members sought a meeting with the council. Their

spokeswoman was Megan Willis who made a heartfelt plea to the Leisure and Amenities Committee to re-consider.

Her words, and her long-standing family ties with the Lido, gave councillors pause for thought. After several more meetings, an experiment was agreed. The Lido could stay open during the winter - if the club ran it. That would save the council an estimated £30,000 a year and allow SLSC members to continue swimming in ice-cold water. Four members of the SLSC became trustees (Steve Adkins, Frank Sims, Jack Snelling and Megan Willis). They are responsible for overseeing all off-season arrangements, including the employment of two life-guards. Five years on, the Lido is still open all the year round.

THE FUTURE

With a steady decline in the number of open-air pools in Britain, the SLSC wants to make sure that Tooting Bec Lido does not become another casualty. In early 1996, it put forward a scheme, initiated by one of the trustees, Steve Adkins, aimed at encouraging more sports groups to use the Lido, especially off-season. The size of the pool (100 x 33 yards) makes it an ideal place for long-distance swimmers,

triathletes and even canoeists to train. Some do so already, but many more could take advantage of an extraordinary facility.

The plans, drawn up by a local firm of architects, Michael Phillips Associates, replace the current entrance with a water sports pavilion. This would provide club facilities and storage space for all groups using the pool while the roof would

A water sports pavilion would provide a meeting place and storage room for all clubs using the Lido. Its roof is intended to be used as a sun terrace.

© Michael Phillips Associates

double up as a sun terrace. A new entrance is planned for the shallow end, making it safer for children and disabled people to come to the Lido. There would also be a heated paddling pool improving the play area for children. All the buildings would be in a distinctive Thirties style.

Wandsworth Council has given its full support to the proposals, but a number of local groups, including the Tooting Commons Management Advisory Committee and the Balham Society, have raised objections. They are concerned about the visual impact on the Common and have cast doubt on the council's long-term intentions. Despite their objections Wandsworth's Planning Committee gave its approval to the proposals at the end of May 1996.

The estimated cost of the project is some £2.5 million. The council, on behalf of the SLSC, intends to submit a bid for lottery funds, possibly through the Sports Council. If successful, this would cover most, but not all, of the cost. The club would still have to raise in excess of £200,000.

One of the key aims of the plans is to retain the unique atmosphere of Tooting Bec Lido. There are few more breathtaking sights than that first view down the length of the pool as you walk in - and even with the entrance at the opposite end, that will be preserved. People arriving for the first time invariably stop and stare in disbelief as if they have just stumbled on some long-hidden treasure.

Many regular swimmers vividly remember their first impressions. One, who was brought as a boy scout to take his 100-yard swimming badge, looked towards the far end of the pool and instinctively thought: 'I'll never be able to swim that far.' Another compares the experience with that conjured up in the children's story, *The Lion, the Witch and the Wardrobe*. 'It was like walking through the wardrobe door into a new and magical world', she says.

Once inside, who can resist the Lido's charms? Its bright colours are warm and welcoming and evoke a sense of seaside fun. The bubbling fountain, and cafe behind, draw you down to the far end to indulge in food and drink or just to sun-bathe on the terrace or, in many cases,

both. The Lido can be a noisy and joyous place on a busy summer's day, yet the same place can inspire calmness and inner peace on a cold winter's day.

Club members, many of whom have been swimming at the Lido for decades, give different reasons for their extraordinary devotion. For some, it is the camaraderie, for others it is the place itself. One says she likes the space. 'It's large enough to accommodate my mood: I can talk with people or go into the water and have my own thoughts.' For a doctor, it's the water itself. 'I like the cold water', he says. 'If I know I have a hard day at work, I like to start off with a swim. It's a big part of my life.' Others believe the cold water has a therapeutic effect - and recent scientific research suggests it may help to overcome depression. One member, though, takes a more philosophical view: 'Cold water is mainly in the mind', he thinks, 'it's never as cold as you imagined.'

Not many would go along with that view. But all, whether occasional dippers or all-year round swimmers, would surely agree that Tooting Bec Lido is a haven in one of the world's biggest cities, where people can ease the stresses and strains of modern city life.

Perhaps the long-serving SLSC captain, William Laws, put it best back in 1930: 'My advice for a long life is: be an open-air swimmer, join our club and have a contented mind.'

93 year old Henry Harvey, the oldest club member. June 1996.